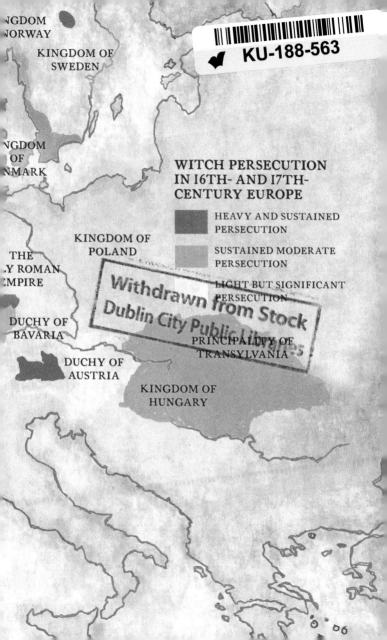

KINGDOM OF
NORWAY

KINGDOM OF
SWEDEN

✔ KU-188-563

KINGDOM
OF
DENMARK

KINGDOM OF
POLAND

THE
HOLY ROMAN
EMPIRE

**WITCH PERSECUTION
IN 16TH- AND 17TH-
CENTURY EUROPE**

HEAVY AND SUSTAINED
PERSECUTION

SUSTAINED MODERATE
PERSECUTION

LIGHT BUT SIGNIFICANT
PERSECUTION

DUCHY OF
BAVARIA

PRINCIPALITY OF
TRANSYLVANIA

DUCHY OF
AUSTRIA

KINGDOM OF
HUNGARY

Series 117

This is a Ladybird Expert book, one of a series of titles for an adult readership. Written by some of the leading lights and outstanding communicators in their fields and published by one of the most trusted and well-loved names in books, the Ladybird Expert series provides clear, accessible and authoritative introductions, informed by expert opinion, to key subjects drawn from science, history and culture.

Every effort has been made to ensure images are correctly attributed, however if any omission or error has been made please notify the Publisher for correction in future editions.

MICHAEL JOSEPH

UK | USA | Canada | Ireland | Australia
India | New Zealand | South Africa

Michael Joseph is part of the Penguin Random House group of companies whose addresses can be found at global.penguinrandomhouse.com

First published 2018
001

Text copyright © Suzannah Lipscomb, 2018

All images copyright © Ladybird Books Ltd, 2018

The moral right of the author has been asserted

Printed in Italy by L.E.G.O. S.p.A.

A CIP catalogue record for this book is available from the British Library
ISBN: 978–0–718–18843–6

www.greenpenguin.co.uk

MIX
Paper from
responsible sources
FSC® C018179

Penguin Random House is committed to a sustainable future for our business, our readers and our planet. This book is made from Forest Stewardship Council® certified paper.

Due Date	Due Date	Due Date

Witches are everywhere

The witch who haunted my youth was Roald Dahl's Grand High Witch. She had square-ended feet without toes, a head as 'bald as a boiled egg', and thought children smelt of dogs' droppings. I found her genuinely terrifying.

Beyond children's stories, the witch remains culturally versatile. In horror films, TV shows (think Melisandre in *Game of Thrones*) and misogynistic depictions of politicians (neither Hillary Clinton nor Theresa May has escaped the charge), the figure of the witch retains her potency to attract and repel. She is a synonym for evil, inversion and desire, and has always been so.

Witchcraft beliefs have been around for thousands of years. In ancient Greece, around 330 BC, alleged witch Theoris of Lemnos was prosecuted for casting incantations and using harmful drugs. Roman poet Tibullus promised his mistress in *c*. 30 BC that he had found a 'truthful witch' to perform 'magic rites' and 'spells' so that her husband would not know she was having an affair. The *Chronicle of AD 354* records the execution in the reign of Tiberius of forty-five sorcerers and eighty-five sorceresses, probably in AD 16/17. In AD 371, Emperor Valentinian forbade haruspicy (divination using the entrails of animals) for harmful ends. Under the French king Clovis, in the early sixth century, those who practised magic were to be fined; Charlemagne ordained in 789 that 'night-witches' should be executed, and Athelstan, King of the Anglo-Saxons (924–39), ordered punishment for anyone casting a spell that led to death.

Witch myths

Witches have always been with us, but there was a moment in history when they were perceived to be especially dangerous. In Europe between 1450 and 1750 large numbers of people were persecuted, prosecuted and executed for being witches. It hadn't happened before, and it hasn't happened since. Why did it happen then?

To answer this, first we need to slay some myths . . .

Myth No. 1: Witches were ducked on stools.

No, that was the punishment for scolds. Witches were swum.

Myth No. 2: All witches were burnt alive.

In England and New England, witches were hanged not burnt; elsewhere, witches were strangled before burning.

Myth No. 3: The medieval Catholic Church was responsible.

No. The vast majority of trials took place in ordinary secular courts. The church's only role was to link popular beliefs to a new idea of a conspiracy of witches headed by the Devil.

Myth No. 4: 'The Church burned at the stake an astounding five million women' (Dan Brown, *The Da Vinci Code*).

It would be astounding if true. In fact, about 90,000 people were prosecuted for witchcraft, and about half of them were executed.

Myth No. 5: The witch-hunt was an attempt to eradicate folk paganism.

There is no credible evidence that convicted witches were pagans or surviving adherents of an old, folk fertility cult.

Magic and the supernatural

In 1500, just about everyone believed in the utter reality and potent power of the supernatural.

Magical practices and 'superstitions' easily mingled with orthodox Christian belief. In 1517, Alonso González de la Pintada described his cure for haemorrhoids: take the sick person to a fig tree, have him kneel facing east with his hat off, bless him, recite a Paternoster and an Ave Maria, then cut down nine figs and take them to a place where neither sun nor smoke can get at them. When the figs have dried out, the piles will be cured.

Magic could be benign. It could also bring good luck – through amulets, carrying herbs or putting shoes in chimneys. It was usual to turn to a local practitioner of beneficent magic (known in England as a 'cunning' man or woman) to seek assistance when things were uncertain or inexplicable.

Cunning folk offered cures for infertility or love potions. They claimed the ability to divine the location of stolen goods and the identity of thieves. A common method was to hang a sieve by shears and nominate the suspects: the sieve would rotate – by magic! – when the guilty party was named.

Magical practitioners believed they could heal sickness – by burying an animal alive, boiling eggs in urine or tying salt and herbs into cows' tails. They also frequently identified sickness as witchcraft, helped the afflicted to name the person responsible and forced the witch to 'heal' their victim (these moments of reconciliation acted as therapy, creating a placebo effect).

Witches, the Devil and the Reformation

But the supernatural could also be malevolent. Witches were said to use magical powers to carry out *maleficium* (harmful magic), causing damage to property and injury or even death to people and animals. To do this, they drew on mysterious, supernatural power, which many believed the witch acquired through a pact with the Devil.

Belief in witches was orthodox doctrine. It was even in the Bible. Exodus 22:18 – 'Thou shall not suffer a witch to live' – offered the ultimate justification for executing witches (although critics questioned the accuracy of the translation).

But the existence of belief in magic and witches is very different from the legal prosecution of witchcraft. So why were witches persecuted?

One possible explanation is that the witch-hunts happened in the aftermath of the Reformation, when there was a crackdown on all forms of 'superstition'. Yet witch-trials happened in both Protestant and Catholic areas, and they weren't directed by one set of believers against the other.

What the Reformation did was create an atmosphere of apocalyptic angst: people believed that they were living in the end days, and this brought the Devil to their minds.

In 1563, cleric Thomas Becon lamented the 'infinite number of wicked angels . . . which without ceasing seek my destruction'. An Essex clergyman wrote in 1587 that 'it is common opinion when there are any mighty winds and thunders with terrible lightnings that the Devil is abroad'.

Satan and his demons stalked the land, engaging the Christian believer in a perpetual struggle.

Elite belief and demonologies

It wasn't just 'common opinion' that thought this. Educated elites did too. They were encouraged to do so by printed books like the famous *Malleus Maleficarum*, or *The Hammer of the Witches*, from 1486. Written principally by a German Dominican monk called Heinrich Kramer (historian Malcolm Gaskill calls him a 'superstitious psychopath'), this book argued that witches existed and that they worked for the Devil.

The *Malleus* was a manual for hunting witches; it included instructions on how to detect and exterminate them. It was full of examples of their satanic evil, such as raising storms, destroying crops, poisoning food, and maiming and killing innocent humans.

It was especially influential because a papal bull (a decree issued by the Pope) from 1484 had stated that witches were heretics who made a pact with Satan. Kramer reproduced the bull at the front of his book to lend the weight of the Church to his work.

A century later, King James VI of Scotland wrote his *Dæmonologie*, an examination of the reality of witches, demons, fairies and werewolves. It is the only book about witches by a reigning monarch. He wrote it to refute sceptics, noting that 'the fearful abounding at this time in this country, of these detestable slaves of the Devil, the witches or enchanters, hath moved me [to write]'.

These two books were among many demonologies printed at this time. As Stuart Clark has argued, demonology was one of the cutting-edge sciences of its day. It created the intellectual foundations of the witch-trials.

The diabolic pact

Demonologists were particularly alarmed by the idea
that witches made pacts with the Devil. Witches – they
believed – beguiled by Satan's promises of wealth and
power, renounced their baptism, offered him their souls and
became his servants. As a sign of the pact, the Devil would
leave a mark 'upon some secret place of their body', which
was insensible to pain.

They also believed that witches gathered at nocturnal
sabbats, where they worshipped the Devil and demonstrated
their obscene obeisance to him by kissing his anus – his
other mouth – in the 'Kiss of Shame'. They engaged in
sexual intercourse with the Devil, and his *incubi* and *succubi*
(demons in male and female form) – the Devil's semen was
'intolerably cold'. Sometimes he took the form of a black
goat or a toad. They also practised cannibalistic infanticide:
Jean Bodin, a French professor of law, public prosecutor
and royal adviser, wrote in his demonology of 1580 that
witches sacrificed their newborns to the Devil and murdered
little children by sticking pins in their heads, before boiling
them to eat their flesh and drink their blood. Above all, they
devoted their attention to raising storms and spoiling crops.

From the demonologies, too, we get the notion that
witches flew to the sabbat, transported through the air by
a mysterious mighty wind, facing backwards on a beast,
on a stick or a pitchfork or, most famously of all, on a
broomstick – a symbol of both domesticity and the phallus.

Such credulity among many of Europe's learned and ruling
elites was a fundamental precondition for the persecution
(even if the demonologists frequently complained that their
colleagues did not take their warnings seriously enough).

The crime of witchcraft

Elite belief in the evil reality of witchcraft and the travesty of the diabolic pact facilitated a crucial shift without which the European witch-hunt could never have happened: witchcraft became a crime.

In England, Acts of Parliament passed in 1542, 1563 and 1604 criminalized witchcraft and black magic became a capital offence. The Scottish Parliament issued a statute against witchcraft in 1563.

Elsewhere in Europe, similar laws were passed. In the Holy Roman Empire (which in judicial terms covered modern Germany and Austria, and some peripheral territories), the Criminalis Constitutio Carolina of 1532 sought to define procedure in witchcraft trials. Over the course of the sixteenth and seventeenth centuries, the rulers of Sweden, Denmark, Norway and Russia also issued edicts against witchcraft. In other states, such as Poland, secular courts increasingly began to hear witch-trials, without any official decree having been passed.

The prosecution and execution of witches was not a frenzied free-for-all nor a crusade by ecclesiastical authorities but a judicial process, handled through secular law courts.

Implementing the law

Although the figures are approximate, the number of trials in each area makes it clear how crucial the legal system was in encouraging or crushing witchcraft prosecutions.

In France, there were comparatively few trials. In the British Isles – except in Scotland in the 1590s and Essex and East Anglia in the 1640s – the persecution was also relatively light: a maximum of 3,000 trials across the period. Similar numbers were tried in Scandinavia and Poland. In Spain, Italy and Portugal, there were plentiful trials, but few executions.

The persecution was worst in the Holy Roman Empire. In the self-governing states of Lorraine and Franche-Comté, prosecutions were high: some 3,000 were executed in the small Duchy of Lorraine alone. But the vast majority of witchcraft prosecutions occurred in the German states, Switzerland and the Low Countries – at least 10,000 in Switzerland and perhaps some 45,000 in the German states.

Whether a suspected witch was likely to be tried – and to die – came down to the authorities' attitude towards evidence.

This can be seen in the German city of Rothenburg-ob-der-Tauber. Numbers here were low – only eighteen cases of witchcraft (involving forty-one suspects) were tried between 1561 and 1652, and of these, nine people were banished and only one was executed.

Why? Because the city council kept strictly to legal definitions of proof, generally presumed innocence and even used torture on accusers to discourage false witness.

The Little Ice Age

Witchcraft had become a crime in law and people believed in magic. But there's a missing link: how did witchcraft beliefs become accusations that became prosecutions?

To understand this, we need to think about the conditions of life: times were a-changing. There were more people than ever before – the population of England rose from 2.5m in 1525 to 4m in 1600 – and the cost of food was multiplying. Inflation had been unknown to previous generations, so it was both shocking and punitive: people found it increasingly difficult to afford bread.

The weather was dire. This period is known as the Little Ice Age – from 1560, the temperature dropped substantially. In 1607, the first Frost Fair was held on the frozen Thames, the ice so thick that people even burnt fires on it.

One in four harvests failed, and that meant hunger. If two or three consecutive harvests failed, it meant severe dearth. In 1594–7, the rain fell incessantly across Europe. Wheat rotted in the fields. The harvests of 1593, 1594, 1596 and 1597 failed. Prices soared, and there was famine.

Add to that plague (which recurred roughly once every sixteen years), influenza, and religious warfare in France, the Netherlands and the Holy Roman Empire.

Finally, changing patterns of land-holding profited the wealthy and impoverished the poor, shifting from medieval customary tenure (fixed, low rents) to contractual tenure (rents fixed by the market, so high that they were called 'rack-rents', as they put the tenant on the rack).

Someone had to be to blame for these apocalyptic conditions.

The dawn of modernity

The peaks of the witch-trials across Europe were in the 1590s, 1620–30s and 1660s, correlating to times of poor harvests, plague and war.

Yet there were also disasters that weren't followed by accusations, and some areas didn't experience such terrible conditions but did try witches.

The causality is not simple, but what is clear is that famine, poverty, war and conflict created the mental and emotional space in which witchcraft accusations could happen, by making people fearful in the face of the instability and uncertainty of life. Not to mention hungry, angry and envious.

Most people lived in small village communities, and depended on each other. They lent, borrowed, gave and forgave. It was the only way to get along. But in tough times, people turn in on themselves. They start to look after number one. A neighbour who would not offer help or charity, who enriched himself by expanding his farm as others were forced to give up theirs, or who begged for handouts when everyone was suffering could foster resentment, bitterness and suspicion.

These feelings were the product of a transition from old to new ways. In grand socio-economic terms, what was happening was a shift towards capitalism. The witch-trials were the blood-red fingers of the dawn of modernity.

The refusal-guilt syndrome

How did a witchcraft accusation occur?

One model of how it might have worked came from historians Alan Macfarlane and Keith Thomas. They linked the rise of witchcraft accusations in English communities with the social and economic changes of the late sixteenth century.

Picture the scene: a poor, elderly widow goes to the door of a richer neighbour to beg for alms. He, feeling stretched and thinking that he's already given enough money to the poor-relief fund, refuses. She scowls and turns away, muttering angrily under her breath. Then his child gets sick or his cow dies, and he thinks that she's cursed him: she's a witch.

Yeoman Henry Cockcrofte told Justices of the Peace in Yorkshire in 1646 that Elizabeth Crossley, 'in evil report for witching', came to his house to beg. She was unhappy with what his wife gave her and muttered something as she left. Later that night, Cockcrofte's infant son mysteriously fell sick, and died three months later. Cockcrofte accused Crossley of witchcraft, and soon other neighbours told similar tales.

The accused witch was generally poor and dependent on others, and often old, female and widowed. She had recently been turned away or inadequately helped by her accuser at a time of need. The accuser felt subconsciously guilty and projected the implicit aggression of his rejection onto the witch, who was assumed to be offended.

It's a persuasive model, but it doesn't explain why guilt manifested itself in accusations of witchcraft.

Why witchcraft?

Our ancestors did not blame every misfortune on witchcraft: only certain unexpected, freakish or unfair circumstances, such as a sudden illness in the previously healthy, a lingering disease, an attack that left a person strangely disabled, or anything untoward involving children, impotence, childbirth or pregnancy.

In Upwell, Norfolk, in 1646, Robert and Katherine Parsons watched their seven-year-old and six-month-old die within three weeks of each other. In an age of high child mortality, they blamed the deaths on their neighbour Ellen Garrison because their children had been in perfect health before they suddenly wasted away and died.

There were two other reasons for suspecting Garrison: the children's deaths had followed a recent argument with her over the sale of a pig, and Garrison had a reputation for sorcery. Katherine Parsons swore that Garrison 'bewitched her children to death and that she hath bin [*sic*] accounted a witch at least 20 years and her mother was so esteemed before her'.

An accusation of witchcraft was not a knee-jerk reaction: the harm needed to be a plausible bewitchment, and there needed to be reasons for suspecting someone. Witch-trials were hard to get going, and there was also the possibility that they would backfire: if you thought someone was a witch, with evil, supernatural powers, the last thing you'd want to do is annoy her.

People may have believed that witches existed, thought people around them to be witches, worried about them and despised them – and still not have acted on their suspicions.

Catalysts and rumours

What was needed for a witch-hunt to happen was a catalyst.

Agnes Browne of Guilsborough in Northamptonshire was 'ever noted to be of an ill nature and wicked disposition, spiteful and malicious, and many years before she died [was] both hated and feared among her neighbours'. Mistress Belcher, a 'godly gentlewoman' of the town, argued with Agnes's daughter, Joan, and hit her. Four nights later, Mistress Belcher experienced pain 'gripping and gnawing her body', and blamed both Joan and her mother, publicly denouncing them as witches. In July 1612, both mother and daughter were found guilty of the bewitchment of Mistress Belcher and hanged on the Abingdon gallows.

It is doubtless significant that Mistress Belcher was a 'godly gentlewoman' – a Puritan – prone to seeing the world in piebald terms and the Devil at work everywhere, but she triggered a witch-trial because there had been a specific event so terrible that it overrode her fears of retribution, and it happened immediately after an altercation with someone long rumoured to be a witch. This combination was the catalyst for a public accusation.

It is likely that in every community there were several suspected witches who were disliked and distrusted by their neighbours for many years before they were accused – if they ever were. A reputation for witchcraft was built up over a long time, through rumour and gossip about remembered slights and crimes. After the judiciary got involved, these affronts were later recalled, and probably embellished, under questioning.

Reputations

A case from Robin Briggs' research on Lorraine demonstrates how a reputation for witchcraft was constructed. In 1619, seven people testified against fifty-five-year-old Maiette Lutschen. They included:

Thirty-eight-year-old Adam, her brother-in-law – ten years earlier, he had woken at night to see Maiette standing by his bed. He called her a witch, dragged her outside and struck her several times. Since then, he hadn't kept animals successfully.

Twenty-four-year-old Nicholas – two years earlier, he'd stolen some peas from Maiette's garden. She spotted him and told him 'she would eat some of his'. Within days he became ill, excreting round worms that looked like peas.

Twenty-six-year-old Barbe – six years earlier, she and her sister had been collecting herbs in Maiette's hemp field. Maiette struck her several times, after which she was ill for three years.

Fifty-year-old Barbe – ten years earlier she'd been Maiette's neighbour. When her bull sickened, Maiette made it a cure, and the next day it died. Barbe's husband complained that the animal had been bewitched and woke in the night to see Maiette standing over him; two days later, his left arm was swollen and painful. Barbe refused to make Maiette's daughter a loaf. Days later, her own daughter disappeared, returning with a mouth black as coal, unable to speak or stand, and died three days later. Maiette 'was the cause of all her misfortune and poverty'.

Maiette was subsequently interrogated under torture, confessed to being a witch and was executed.

The stereotype of the witch

As a fifty-five-year-old woman, Maiette Lutschen conformed to the stereotype of a witch, described in 1584 by sceptic Reginald Scot as 'women which be commonly old, lame, bleary-eyed, pale, foul, full of wrinkles, poor, sullen, superstitious . . . lean and deformed . . . miserable wretches . . . so odious unto all their neighbours, and so feared, as few dare offend them'.

The witch of the imagination was a poor, elderly crone. People thought that witches were miserable, ugly and malevolent hags, often with some physical deformity – a crippled leg, hunchback or harelip.

In practice, alleged witches were predominantly middle-aged or older. Most witches in Essex (of those for whom ages are recorded) were between fifty and seventy years old. In the Geneva trials of 1571–2, the average age was sixty. In Lorraine, the majority were between forty and seventy.

During severe panics, stereotypes became less relevant. In 1611 in Ellwangen, Germany, seventy-year-old Barbara Rüfin's confession under torture sparked a ferocious craze in which around 430 men and women were executed, including priests and a judge who had protested about his wife's arrest. The most terrible deviation from the stereotype was children: at Würzburg in 1627–9, more than forty children were executed as witches. Child witches were also named in the Basque country in 1609–11 and Mora, Sweden, in 1669 (where children were among those testifying too).

Still, the fact remains that most executed witches were over the age of forty-five – and most of them were women.

Was it a woman-hunt?

In most places in Europe, over 70 per cent of accused witches were women. In some places – Basel, Namur (in modern Belgium), Hungary, Wielkopolska in Poland, and Essex in England – the figure rises to over 90 per cent.

In 1975, radical feminist Andrea Dworkin published a book called *Woman Hating* in which she described the witch-hunts as 'gynocide' and a 'woman's holocaust', although she overestimated the numbers killed by a factor of 1,000. Anne Llewellyn Barstow gave her book *Witchcraze* the subtitle 'Our Legacy of Violence Against Women', by which she meant men's. In these readings, female witches were the passive victims of the male establishment.

Recent feminist scholars – Diane Purkiss, Deborah Willis and Lyndal Roper – have challenged such work, pointing to women's role as accusers as well as victims, and attending to more subtle questions around psychoanalysis, ageing, female socialization and motherhood. Robin Briggs states: 'What we need to explain is why women were particularly vulnerable to witchcraft accusations, not why witchcraft was used as an excuse to attack women.'

The *Malleus* demonstrates the most extreme misogynistic beliefs about women that made them susceptible to accusation: women 'are more credulous, and . . . therefore [the Devil] rather attacks them . . . women are naturally more impressionable . . . they have slippery tongues'. Above all, a woman 'is more carnal than a man'.

Like their foremother, Eve, women were thought to be weaker than men, more quickly tempted to sin and therefore more easily seduced by the Devil.

Anti-mothers

Such notions attached especially easily to older women.

Marriage, childbirth and pregnancy were celebrated. Lyndal Roper argues that a culture of motherhood meant that large-hipped, big-bellied and full-breasted women were thought desirable, because they were fertile.

Many suspected witches were not. Visually, witches were depicted as shrivelled-up, sagging crones. Unable now to have children, perhaps widowed, but still insatiable, they copulated with the Devil and enviously attacked fertile mothers and young children. The witch was the anti-mother.

Roper suggests that the crucial characteristic of witches was not just that they were old but that they were no longer fertile. Menopausal and post-menopausal women were disproportionally represented among the accused and executed.

In 1593 in Nördlingen, Germany, Margretha Knorz went to stay with Madalena Mincker, supporting her when she had a child by bringing her gifts of wine, apples and milk. Later, they rowed over money, and Knorz told the young mother she would regret it. Three weeks later, the child grew ill and became 'quite lame and crippled in hands and feet'.

A century later in Augsburg, eighty-year-old Ursula Grön was denounced as a witch and subjected to torture (she was tied to a bench and whipped). She was accused of injuring young children, because she had offered them apples and pieces of bread that were said to be poisoned. Grön stated under questioning that 'people don't like old women to give children things'. Older women were easily cast as bitter and envious enough to maim and kill innocents.

Male witches

Yet, across Europe, 20–25 per cent – at least one in five – accused witches were male.

In some places the numbers were greater still. In Lorraine, 28 per cent of prosecuted witches were male; in Finland, half were men. In Estonia and Moscow, the proportion of men accused was 60 and 68 per cent respectively; in Normandy, male witches outnumbered female three to one. Most strikingly, in Iceland in 1625–85, 92 per cent of accused witches were men.

There were various culture-specific reasons for this. In Normandy and Russia, many accused male witches were itinerant: vagrants, folk healers, shepherds. Vagrants were seen as frightening and dangerous deviants, operating outside the normal hierarchical order. In Lorraine, nearly half of all male witches were related to a previously condemned witch.

Above all, though, the reason was that while women were more likely to succumb to diabolic temptation, men too could be morally and spiritually weak.

A pamphlet from 1642, *Fearefull Newes from Coventry*, tells of musician Thomas Holt, who made a Faustian pact on his deathbed, selling himself to the Devil. Satan reneged on his side of the bargain, however: Holt left a chest 'which after his death was opened and found filled to the top with gold . . . but being once touched it fell to dust'.

Even more gruesomely, in 1589, Peter Stumpf of Bedburg confessed, under torture, to using black magic to become a werewolf and to eating two pregnant women and fourteen children, including his own son. He was brutally executed.

Proof

It is no coincidence that Stumpf confessed to such lurid crimes after torture.

Torture was not officially used in England, where major crimes were tried at the regular Assizes, with the verdict given by juries, sometimes after putting the suspected witch through an ordeal.

In his *Dæmonologie*, James VI recommended a 'swimming' ordeal for witches: stripped and tied up, the suspected witch would be dunked in a river or pond to see whether she sank or floated. If innocent, she would sink and be pulled out by a rope. If guilty, she would float, the water itself proclaiming judgement: 'the water shall refuse to receive [those . . .] that have shaken off them the sacred water of baptism'.

Most of Europe, however, used a different criminal procedure: the inquisitorial system of justice. Here, crimes were investigated by court officials, who privately interrogated suspects and witnesses, and kept written records of depositions. Guilt had to be proved by evidence, normally two eyewitness testimonies or a confession.

Ironically, it was this rational, evidence-based inquisitorial procedure that best facilitated witch-trials. French royal prosecutor Jean Bodin argued that witchcraft was an exceptional crime in which normal, stringent rules of evidence should be waived: 'in an occult case . . . it is not necessary to observe the circumstances required in other more visible and evident crimes, because the proof of this particular crime is very difficult'.

If the only reliable witnesses were witches themselves, then they had to be made to confess.

Torture

This meant torture, used discriminately during interrogation in the belief that pain was a guarantor of truth.

Thumb-screws, head-screws and leg-clamps were used to compress parts of the body painfully. Dr Fian, a Scottish witch, suffered the clamps in the 1590s and it was reported that 'his legs were crushed and beaten together as small as might be, and the bones and flesh so bruised that the blood and marrow spouted forth in great abundance'.

Alternatively, the body could be agonizingly stretched, through strappado (in which the arms were tied behind the back and the person raised off the ground by the wrists), the rack (far the commonest form of torture) or hanging by the thumbs. In Scotland, a 'turcas' was used to tear out suspects' nails. In Germany, witches were strapped to iron chairs, which were heated from below, or were stretched and whipped on a bench. Some suspects were tortured to death.

Research into modern-day victims of torture by psychologist Nimisha Patel suggests that beyond sheer pain, torture causes intense shock and fear, temporary lapses of consciousness, disorientation and confusion, involuntary urination and defecation (and the consequent humiliation), and traumatic amnesia.

In Scotland and in England (outside the law, by self-appointed 'Witchfinder General' Matthew Hopkins in East Anglia and Essex during the 1640s), sleep deprivation was used. This also produces disorientation and confusion, plus increased suggestibility, delirium, hallucinations and cognitive impairment – it becomes difficult to respond coherently, make decisions and know what is real and what is not.

Confessions

The cumulative effect of interrogatory torture is the physical and psychological breaking of a person.

This means that rather than eliciting truth, torture was very likely to produce anything but. In the face of intense and prolonged pain, most people will do and say whatever is necessary to survive. Under torture, people come to believe what they are told. Their ability to reason is eroded. Their perception of reality is distorted. An interrogator repeatedly asking leading questions would have found that witches' confessions reflected very exactly his own preoccupations and fascinations – that witches made diabolic pacts, met in covens, had sex with demons – because those were the scenarios he posed.

Yet there are instances of people confessing to being a witch even when torture was not used. Why?

There must have been some people who believed themselves to be witches, and who had genuinely tried to summon demons, curse their neighbours or murder with magic.

Some of those accused – often lonely outsiders with various disabilities – may have been mentally unstable or psychologically disturbed. A few may have ingested narcotics. Maybe others, faced with the prospect of profound social isolation if released, made a rational choice to face death.

But the confessions we cannot explain away require us to engage more deeply with the desires and dreams of accused witches.

Fantasy and despair

As well as revealing the fantasies of interrogators, confessions offer an insight into those of the accused: companionship, sex, power, freedom from hunger, wealth, revenge and hope.

In 1645, Mary Skipper confessed to becoming a witch when 'the Devil appeared to her in the shape of a man after her husband's death and told [her] if she would enter a covenant with him he would pay her debts and . . . would carry her to heaven . . . and she would never want'. Here was the promise of relief from poverty, debt and the endless toil of life.

Eighty-year-old Elizabeth Clarke said that the Devil, in the shape of 'a tall, proper, black haired gentleman', had visited her bed for six or seven years, always saying, 'Besse I must lye with you'. Another widow said that Satan came 'in the shape of a handsome young gentleman with yellow hair and black clothes and oftentimes lay with her'. The elderly often suffer from 'skin hunger'. Those starved of human touch may have mistaken their guilty dreams of being desired and caressed for reality.

Or perhaps they fantasized about hope. Malcolm Gaskill has written about Margaret Moore, a poor, lonely woman who had watched three of her four children die. As the last lay sick, she heard a demon calling to her, 'Mother, Mother, good sweet Mother, let me in,' and offering to save the life of her remaining child in exchange for her soul. In despair, she may have imagined offering the only thing she could, in return for her child's life. She was hanged in Ely in the summer of 1647.

Endings

The year 1692 saw the most sensational case of witchcraft in America, in Salem. Between 144 and 185 people were named as witches, 59 were tried and 19 were executed. The first witches to be named fitted the standard model – quarrelsome, female misfits – but, over time, the victims – a group of adolescent girls manifesting signs of possession – named more candidates. The authorities, however, quickly lost confidence, stopped the trials and released the prisoners.

In Europe, witchcraft prosecutions were starting to dry up. The timescale for this varied enormously. The last execution for witchcraft in the Dutch Republic (1609) occurred well before some of the major witch-hunts elsewhere in Europe. In England, the last witch to be executed was Alice Molland, hanged in Devon in 1685. Scotland's last was Janet Horne in 1722.

The end of the witch-trials resulted from a changing intellectual, legal, economic and religious climate. Most importantly, judicial authorities started to insist on stricter evidentiary requirements for proving witchcraft than before. This meant more cases ended without convictions. At the Home Circuit Assizes in 1660–1701, all forty-eight witchcraft indictments ended in acquittal. In the same year as Salem, a jury in Kent acquitted a group of witches because there was 'no other material evidence against them but their own confessions'.

Declining convictions, in turn, made witchcraft less plausible. By 1700 witch-trials were rare. The last occurred in the 1770s and 1780s in Poland, Spain and Switzerland. Europe's last official witch, Anna Göldi, was executed in Glarus in 1782.

Witch-hunts are everywhere

The law followed practice. Trials gradually petered out and, subsequently, witchcraft legislation was repealed or reformed: in France in 1682, Prussia in 1714, England in 1735–6, Russia in 1770, Poland in 1776 and Sweden in 1779. But a decline in witchcraft trials did not necessarily mean a decline in belief in witches, magic and the supernatural.

Worldwide, witch-hunts have occurred far more recently. There were 200 lynchings of suspected witches in South Africa in 1985–95. In the Democratic Republic of Congo in 2001, there were, officially, 843 killings by witch-hunters in Ituri Province within a fortnight (unofficial figures suggest 2,000–4,000 dead). Many of those brutally murdered were killed for possessing onions – the Devil's vegetable.

The religious police in Saudi Arabia created an Anti-Witchcraft Unit in 2009 and in 2011 the Saudi courts ordered the beheading of two people for having 'committed the practice of witchcraft and sorcery'.

In 2012, a Congolese couple living in London were convicted at the Old Bailey for murdering fifteen-year-old Kristy Bamu, because they thought he was a witch. In 2013, a mob in Papua New Guinea burnt alive a twenty-year-old woman called Kepari Leniata as a witch.

There have been similar witch-hunts in Nepal, Columbia, Indonesia, Nigeria . . . In 2014, the *New York Times* reported that witch-hunting is on the rise, with thousands killed every year.

Understanding why people are persecuted for witchcraft matters now, more than ever.

Further reading

I am especially indebted to the work of Robin Briggs, Malcolm Gaskill, Brian P. Levack, Lyndal Roper, James Sharpe and Keith Thomas.

Wolfgang Behringer, *Witches and Witch-Hunts: A Global History* (Polity Press, 2004)

Robin Briggs, *Witches and Neighbours: The Social and Cultural Context of European Witchcraft* (Blackwell Publishing, 1996)

Robin Briggs, *The Witches of Lorraine* (Oxford University Press, 2007)

Robin Briggs (trans. and ed.), *Lorraine Witchcraft Trials* (http://witchcraft.history.ox.ac.uk)

Stuart Clark, *Thinking with Demons: The Idea of Witchcraft in Early Modern Europe* (Clarendon Press, 1997)

Ronald Hutton, *The Witch: A History of Fear, from Ancient Times to the Present* (Yale University Press, 2017)

Malcolm Gaskill, *Witchfinders: A Seventeenth-Century English Tragedy* (John Murray, 2005)

Malcolm Gaskill, *Witchcraft: A Very Short Introduction* (Oxford University Press, 2010)

Brian P. Levack, *The Witch-Hunt in Early Modern Europe* (Longman, 1995)

Alan Macfarlane, *Witchcraft in Tudor and Stuart England: A Regional and Comparative Study* (Routledge, 1999)